The Man at Home

The Man at Home

Michael Heffernan

The University of Arkansas Press
Fayetteville · London
1988

Designer: Chiquita Babb
Typeface: Linotron 202 Cochin
Typesetter: G&S Typesetters, Inc.
Printer: Thomson-Shore, Inc.
Binder: John H. Dekker & Sons, Inc.

The paper used in this publication meets the minimum
requirements of the American National Standard for
Permanence of paper for Printed Library Materials
Z39.48-1984. ∞

Library of Congress Cataloging-in-Publication Data
Heffernan, Michael, 1942-
    The man at home.
    Bibliography: p.
    I. Title.
PS3558.E4133M3   1988   811'.54   88-10597
ISBN 1-55728-022-3 (alk. paper)
ISBN 1-55728-042-8 (pbk. : alk. paper)

For Kathy

ACKNOWLEDGMENTS

The author thanks the editors of the following journals in which these poems first appeared, sometimes in earlier versions:

The American Poetry Review: "The Neighborhood Crazyman Talks to the President on the Eve of the Libyan Raids" and "Saturday"

The Chariton Review: "All That You Can Be," "Babies, Babies," "The Dancing Ground," "Halfway in the Journey," and "In Prospect of Eden"

College English: "Jim's Cafe"

Colorado Review: "The Ad Hoc Committee" and "The Postcard"

The Georgia Review: "Liberty"

The Gettysburg Review: "In the Forum at Lugdunum" and "The Journey to Brindisi"

Hubbub: "Fishing Cow Creek during the Grenada Invasion"

The Iowa Review: "Blackbirds," "The House of God," "Litany against the Bellyache, Upon St. Brigid's Day," "The Manhood of Ireland," "Reading Aquinas," and "Willow"

Memphis State Review: "Answer the Phone"

The Midwest Quarterly: "Amid a Place of Stone," "The Back Road to Arcadia," "A Boyhood among the Cannibals," "The Funeral," "Lines from the Interior," "Living Room," "Manchild," "The Misery," "The Missing Link," "Slugs," and "St. Anthony Brings St. Paul the Hermit a Cloak in Which to Bury Him"

The Missouri Review: "The Sun Comes out in South Haven"

Poetry Northwest: "At the Tire Fire at the Landfill," "Here Lies the Heart," "Lacrimae Rerum," "Presidents," and "What I Did on my Vacation"

Poetry NOW: "The Dream of '43"

The Quarterly: "The Morning Mail"

The completion of this book was assisted by a fellowship grant from the National Endowment for the Arts.

CONTENTS

Go home to thy friends, and tell them how great things the Lord hath done for thee, and hath had compassion on thee.

— Mark 5:19

LINES FROM THE INTERIOR

— to Tom O'Leary

First I was going to say I think my numbers
have grown so numb they're frozen tight with rime
beneath which every nerve inside me slumbers

as they've been slumbering now for a long time,
especially since I've all but dissipated
down to a torpid squalor; but the rhyme

you mailed me Monday got me motivated
to scribble something for the joy of it,
though I'll admit my wit's exasperated

by certain things neglecting to go right
that once I might have bent my brains to fix
when ample forces kept me wild and wet

that now am winded pulling up my socks,
gone flaccid at the loins, loose at the knees,
and so plush in the guts my carcass looks

about to burst with griefs and grievances —
the daily round of consternations — taking
up room amid my noontime reveries

and, in this message to my great friend, breaking
about me like a soundless surf, because
that silence that the mind is always making

from grim confusions must pronounce a pause —
in which the blessed soul alone rejoices
by some diversion of the natural laws —

proposing nothing to restore those spaces
back to a shape for praising. So I start
stitching along by fitful bits and pieces

of seemly rhyming, to arouse the heart
most mightily with something I can shout
among my bricks and beams when I'm apart

from all the brainless wonders hereabout.
A good thing I have friends like you, O'Leary,
to keep me mindful of the life without.

My countrymen are nuts, the times are scary,
and Kansas is a godforsaken place.
People are even meaner in Missouri.

                    *

A few days later I return to this.
Somehow my blood's more supple than it was
a couple verses back. The wind, I guess,

curling the curtains, can amend my views.
Nine in the morning, Sunday, 65
degrees, the Ides of March. I work outdoors

mending a redbud in the frontyard. I've
also a broken sewer-tile round back,
the main drain, 6 feet down. I wouldn't give

the expeditious plumber up the block
the kind of money that they ask you for,
so I taught myself such things, divulged a knack

for ells and wire nuts, learned to hang a door,
and even built a splendid place on top
of our part of the house, on the 3rd floor —

the former ballroom — where a mad misanthrope
dwells with his lady, though we've seldom seen
or heard them for that matter, while the dope-

fiend in the basement, normally supine,
will now and than convince some corn-fed girl
that he's the Bodhisattva of Mary Jane.

The latter makes him happy, as a rule,
opens him toward his elemental body,
old as the stones, one with the cow and squirrel.

Much beyond these, the facts in his grasp are spotty:
his plot to trip The System by some trick
eludes him — says he clean forgot — a shoddy

example of what this place calls a freak,
devoid of nuance, naive to the core,
vacant of everything that makes men quick,

and there he vegetates under our floor.
Yet we're a glad house otherwise: two dogs,
three boys, eleven fishes — one a poor

gruesome plecostimus who only lugs
his dreadful self around when he's awake
or dozes like a troll among some crags.

*

Next morning, and I'm all but out of luck
with this epistle. Maundering on thus far,
I'm lost for words to wind around this lock-

step neofascist strophe and still more
or less unfold a fabric of events
roughly resembling those which we endure

in this our life. I'd wanted to dispense
some oddments from the lives of fishes, plus
more details of the house we live in, hence

broadening somewhat your fantasy of us,
trailing in with the truth about our johns —
taped with quotations from Lucretius —

our balconies, our broad front porch that runs
around three sides and whose roof needs repair,
but something rises on me withershins

to let some mean thing enter, let the air
admit one hungry thing, usher it in
where I sit plangent in a rapt despair,

gazing against the blankness fist to chin
as murkier the deeps that growl around me grow,
and I within them raising my own small din,

clamoring after famine with my tale of woe.
How do I manage on a given day
to give the whole truth over? Off I go

bravely bewildered as I make my way,
weighty with intimations, towards another
casual disaster, dingy disarray,

or some such raggedness, though I'd much rather
emptily ambulate through what went wrong
than tell O'Leary everything I saw there.

So I bring all this home, this overlong
evasion of the rugged dark I prowl
the edges of, in spite of which I've wrung

syllable out of meager syllable
the whole week long, to this appointed close,
wishing I knew the word most musical
to nudge another Monday from its dumb repose.

THE BACK ROAD TO ARCADIA

The tiny thought that breached the inner tissue
of a brain beleaguered as mine was
said that the other world could be drawn in
from the dream inside the neighborhood,
which was the same kind of dream as the ones
that flicker through a man's mind at night,
regardless of all that daybreak with its birds.
Then the tree chirped and the light grew thin.
The backs of paving stones were black as beetles.
I had come by the back road to Arcadia.
Pin oaks and mimosas held up redbuds by the arms.
A pair of grackles scraped the sky and plummeted.
Dogpen yapped to dogpen. Forsythia
splattered the white wall of the toolshed.

READING AQUINAS

Maybe what Thomas means when he says grace
is its own prerequisite, or words to that effect,
has something to do with these sweet tides of joy
one feels now and then in the bottom of the breast
while crossing the street against the light
or watching children at play or cats leaping around
or birds leaving the branches quivering under them
and the stillness of the branches afterwards.
Maybe it's times like these that Thomas means,
though I'm in doubt on this and other issues,
including the one correlative idea
about how the Divine Essence cannot be known
to a person who is still in the body, except
"in dreams or alienations of the senses,"
which is a truly wonderful consideration
coming from a corpulent 13th-century Dominican —
and grace again is an explicit component here:
"the images in the imagination are divinely formed,"
involving "the infusion of gratuitous light,"
Thomas having elsewhere carefully explained
how it takes grace to prepare oneself for grace,
as in that sudden shower one afternoon last summer,
like a sparkling airy essence of divine light,
I found a portly African in a Hawaiian shirt
baptizing himself in the street and marveling:
"I couldn't help myself! This rain is exquisite!" —
the two of us finally standing face to face,
one of us an angel in a shirt of flowers,
the other blessed as he could be because of that.

WHAT I DID ON MY VACATION

In the dream about Edward G. Robinson
the chauffeur that drove us into Detroit
had an attitude about work that I liked.
I realized that Edward G. Robinson
was one of those visitations in the psyche
through which the dreamer recognizes his need
to shape the collective consciousness —
all of which seemed straightforward enough
right down to the mouse-gray limousine
with plush gray carpet and the dapper little man
in the black homburg to whom I addressed
a lengthy digression on the vulnerability
his villains often convey, despite their cruelty —
but it was the casual chauffeur I liked best
who told us we would have to wait awhile
until he got the pizza stains off his vest,
which he did by frequently applying his thumb
wrapped in a handkerchief laden with spit —
and besides you don't pay me enough to do this, Boss,
even though I like my work, my situation in life,
and you too, Boss, he said — and then we were off
up a precipitous avenue into downtown Prague
to meet Mr. Robinson's jeweller about a set
of amethyst cufflinks for the President's funeral.
I woke up outside of Blue Eye, Arkansas,
a place conducive to elegant fantasies,
despite the luxuriance of local ingenuities
such as the treeful of gourdlike purple jugs
and juglike purple gourds next to the yard

full of '56 Crown Victorias (Not 4 Sale)
and the half-finished granite wall and tower
like a 14th-century friary beside Hiway 13
available from Strout Realty for the highest bid
from the craziest individual in these parts
who had evidently failed to materialize
since this time last year when the same edifice
was also for sale. Some of us call this home
and some of us also go home when the time comes,
which hadn't happened yet, which was why I was here,
dreaming of amethyst cufflinks and the jeweller
whose name was, oh yes, Grigori Komikapoulou,
and he and Little Caesar spoke French to one another,
thinking I couldn't understand them, but the one said:
this man over here desires only to associate himself
with those he discerns to be the gods of his age;
and the other said: the President is with
the Corsicans, the harlots, and the Friars Minor,
all of whom pray for the repose of his soul —
and this man over here is going home soon, in his direction,
and I in mine, to where the gods do come from,
though not as he or any of us discerns them.
That place wasn't big enough for all of us,
so off we went in the mouse-gray limousine
to find our way to the train station there in Prague,
the Michigan Central Depot in Blue Eye, Arkansas.

PRESIDENTS

What a joy to climb into bed
being the President of the United States
knowing that probably countless thousands
of even your non-psychotic fellow citizens
are dreaming about you all over the republic.
From Fescue Meadows, Oregon,
to Utility Mills, Massachusetts,
they keep dreaming about you
and your good looks.
At a remote substation in the Valley of Fire,
Assistant Inspector Lloyd E. Towner, Jr.,
has fallen asleep
in a green and yellow lawn-chair
in the only pool of shade
behind the only building in southeast Nevada.
He is dreaming of Anasazi demons
with enormous hands and feet
and penises like snub-nosed revolvers
and testicles brassy as spittoons
and faces full of clacking tongues
that tell him: Inform the President
that we are ready
to extinguish the Evils
he names for us one by one.
In the next frame it is 1948 again.
It is Mrs. Sterling's class in kindergarten.
We have just completed our versions
of George Washington causing the daily war
in purple crayon on slick pieces of paper.

LIVING ROOM

Christmas Eve at Beitzinger's Hardware
John & Phil had bourbon in the backroom for the customers
along with a cooker full of braised raccoon.

I would have eaten some, only Bill Allen,
who was in there replumbing his toilet,
said This coon is a little blue,

and John had referred to cooking it long enough
to get the strangeness out.
So I drank my bourbon and stepped into the light

on Broadway and went next door to buy
Kathy a wristwatch from Bud Benelli,
who was delighted to see me buy something for a change.

The great thing is, I thought,
that down here in the real world nobody's gods win
and nobody's demons either.

Which is why Phil had placed that poor beast's forepaw
on a piece of hardcrust bread
and laid it in the scalepan where they weigh the nails

and Uncle Bud had seen fit that she should come
into the living room with that watch on
dancing to something on the radio.

ALL THAT YOU CAN BE

I flung imagination forth and saw
what life was like in Dacia in the 1st Century B.C.
while the Legions were pulling up stakes against
hordes of primordial white-trash in dogskin overalls.
This was in the garden in the chaise lounge
before coming up attic to tap this out
on the old low-tech Underwood Noiseless.
When I'm in the backyard I dream about the attic,
and when I am up attic I dream about the backyard.
Is anybody out there getting this?
This is like a letter from Quintus Horatius
in the age of Ronaldus Africanus
just lately returned in triumph from his wars.
Kathy has gone upstreet with the three boys,
none of them big enough yet to kill for Christ
or Merrill Lynch. I notice the flamboyant
pair of blossoming redbuds on the berm
across the street while Mick in his white shoes
traipses around the corner dragging a stick,
and I am happy and sad enough at once
to weep for my country and my neighborhood,
but it is Sunday afternoon in the world's garden,
no time for tears of either sorrow or joy,
and everything happens at random anyway —
we found this out, we made this obvious
after sampling thousands of photographic plates —
and as Horace says you're only as good as your friends.
I am going to New York City in a few weeks
to check in on some people I haven't seen

since the Dark Ages — just to be doing this
at this time, at such a time as this,
to make some sense of where they've taken themselves,
in the light, or lack of it, of where I've gone
likewise in the last ten fifteen years.
No doubt I'll look and talk like the Country Mouse
which is all right with me. I can tell you
I have no shame about the place I keep
out here in the provinces. This is my Sabine villa
on a backstreet in a backwater in Kansas.
Tell people in New York you are from Kansas
and they look at you and say I never met
anyone from Kansas, you are my first Kansan.
No, I tell them, actually I am *the*
first Kansan — I am the Governor of Kansas —
and frequently I'm convinced they do believe it.
Mornings I lie awake and look at treetops
and wonder what it was like on the Frontier,
the one with Dacia or with Crazy Horse,
in the days before radar-unfriendly aircraft
and ships that can kill in all directions at once.
I listen to the noiselessness and watch
retarded jaybirds hopping out of the eaves
after what look like little black butterflies
amid the *pock pock pock* of Bruce Pucinski's
basketball in his driveway. *Hoc, hoc vita est:*
It is good to be here as one of the denizens.
Some things are better left to the populace.

13

ANSWER THE PHONE

Monday morning there was a polyp on his mind
& with it a vision of the Lord of Colon Cancer
announcing on the Nightly News that Good
Shit was an object of Happy Life, or possibly

pain-free constipation. Bring me your tired
your poor old lonely enervated bliss-seeker
& I'll show you a polyp masquerading as a man.
Consciousness does not breed joy. *Thou God*

Seest Me said the legend over Elizabeth Taylor's bed
in *Suddenly, Last Summer.* That can't be true.
A man wakes up with the dream still going on
where he is reaching for the top of his mother's dresser

& touching, not her jewel-box as usual,
nor his baby-picture next to the cup full of hatpins,
but Sebastian's bone-white porcelain typewriter
on which he prepared the fair copy of his last

Summer Poem. Beside it a filing cabinet
is overflowing with rough drafts
of that novel he had been working on all that year
about the androgynous hockey player. In walks

the ex-wife, who last appeared as the shadow's
girl Friday in *Bad Times in Bogalusa,* & before
she lifts off her dress the phone rings. Crown
Prince Polyp of Thrace is calling

from Ludlum's Laundromat. He is in town
seeking his throne, & if not that
a stranger's bed to lay his head in,
the ex-wife's will do. They sputter

up Broadway in her mauve Saab. The vanity plate
reads POLLY P, as a broken exhaust pipe
makes sparks on the pavement & the Lord's one
good eye is where the sun would be.

THE MISERY

Obviously I'd like to help you. The deathrate
    from this type of dysfunction is fifteen
out of every hundred cases. Among the rest
    another forty suffer serious
and frequently untreatable debility,
    mainly of the central nervous system,
with ancillary symptoms, such as hearing-loss,
    partial to total blindness, speech defects,
or impotence, while the remaining forty-five
    will experience likewise permanent
though minor maladies: premature loss of hair,
    post-adolescent skin eruptions, boils,
and other chronic non-gonococcal lesions
    on the genitals, along with constant
milky discharge in the inguinal area,
    which will require the daily use of creams
and compresses (salt baths are typically helpful),
    but once again, I'm afraid, all of these
are incurable conditions which will consign
    the patient to a lifetime of heartbreak.
Naturally, I'd like to help you, as I said,
    and you can be sure I would if I could,
but where's the point in trying to set aright what
    Nature herself wishes to keep awry?
I always end up convincing myself the Plan
    must be a good one or it couldn't be
a plan to start with — and how could any of us
    manage without a plan, infirmity
or no infirmity? I look to a future
    (no doubt with something of a mystical

16

impulse on my part) when all of humankind's most
    fearsome disorders of mind and body
can be plainly apprehended and accepted
    as part of the routine of misery
that has always been the case, and always will be,
    in the Scheme-of-Things of the Universe.
At present this is the basis of my concern
    that you not task your mind too much for now
with pointless contemplation of what can happen.
    You'll only worsen a situation
that is already as bad as it wants to be,
    which won't be fair to you or your loved ones.
Meantime, consider the great mortal sufferers
    in all the ages. You are what they were.

JIM'S CAFE

My father got his brother Mike a job
at the DeSoto plant on the East Side
in the late 30s. This was some time before
a room at Mrs. Heller's had come vacant.
Her daughter took one look at my father,
when he was downstairs making a phonecall,
and married him a few months later on.
They're wearing sheepish grins in the wedding picture
I have beside my grandmother's down the hall.
They slept in the master bedroom after that,
Mr. Heller having died some years before.
Uncle Mike couldn't take the assembly line
and had a nervous breakdown at the plant.
They called over the men in the white jackets
who had to wrestle him off to a padded cell
which he took and destroyed with his bare hands.
They couldn't get him to be civilized
so off they carried him back to Indiana,
thanks to the money Uncle Billy sent,
for treatment at the local hospital
before they transferred him to Madison
down by the Ohio River on a hill,
where his brothers visited from time to time
and brought him picnic lunches in a basket
to eat out on the lawn between the buildings.
Later on there was nothing else to do
but let him go home to Montgomery.
After a while he opened a cafe
on Highway 50, with a poker game
in back, numbers, a couple slot machines,
and his wife Geneva, whom the men called Jim,
puffing Pall Malls and wiping off the tables.

THE NEIGHBORHOOD CRAZYMAN
TALKS TO THE PRESIDENT
ON THE EVE OF THE LIBYAN RAIDS

I think I need to give the President
the poem I wrote about the possums' eyes
that watched me from a swamp beside the road
one night when I was driving with the Devil.
They were just little lights. They looked like money
somebody threw at me as we went by,
only, as soon as I went after it,
the money was all gone, it had disappeared.
It must have been a fire that came and burned it.
Even the big half dollars were turned to steam.
And then it was just me and the dark again
along that road that took us through the swamp,
me and the Devil. Mr. President,
I wrote a better poem about barnacles
and big rocks by the ocean. I was alone.
Even the Devil didn't know me then.
I saw a dime down in a little pool
between two rocks with weeds and barnacles.
I climbed down on my knees to bring it up.
I fell and cut my hands on the barnacles.
A bunch of gulls jumped up and then they flew.
Then I was by myself. My hands were bleeding.
I held them in the air to make the sting
fly up the way the gulls did and be gone.
The sting went up like black bombs going back
to where they came from. They were standing still
like crosses in the sky, hundreds of crosses
nailed to the sky. I couldn't move. I waited
for God to come, or Jesus, or the Devil.
I waited for you to come but you weren't there.

MANCHILD

Green thickets hiding me from all but joy
or night alarms that raised me up too far
toward enmity against particular
embodiments of the everlasting Why
left me at last with slumber in a dry
confusion. Thunder, birdsong, rainfall were
divine ideas of an earlier
redemption in the skin. I was a boy
of seven underneath. Multiple sins
against the sacred idiom of desire
cried out to be expunged. This joy I mention,
it was like candy-drops in little tins,
like tiny coals nesting inside the fire,
the look of larks taking a turn in sunshine.

What did you mean by that, madman? Whatever
it ends up saying is the thing I mean.
I mean to say precisely what the lover
says when he finds beloved words again
to make beloved talk for his beloved.
Nobody's reason for the things I do —
as I continue moving in the vivid
kingdom the likes of me can hardly know —
bears any likeness to the things I see.
You call it what you will — call it insane —
call it a temperamental vanity
of heart and head — call it the utmost sign
of something rampant in the poor man's soul
and ugly as a rat in a sewer hole.

But these were larks and these were elms as well
and tulips yellow, pink and lavender
and here were squirrels facing each other
around a plumtree by the garden wall
and yes, I kept on thinking, yes, of all
the other lovely things to tell to her
including certain wonders that never were
except in nightsongs once the quiet fell
and I could listen to the silences
between words, where the words were hidden fast.
And when this knowledge came on me at last
that she might hear me if I said she was
the one bad woman that I ever knew
worthy of praising, maybe that would do.

But what is this you're up to, madman, now?
But me no buts, Alonzo, said the Friar
in green organza riding his gravid cow
with gaudy yellow horns that read DESIRE
on banners purply curling from them both.
One might do worse than ride a cow's backside,
crowed joyous Harry unfolding his face beneath
two eyes that roamed a virginal forehead
winsome and white as lily-petals fallen
upon a lawn where languid ladies strayed.
Let me be lethal, let me be sullen,
the captious Captain bragged: Nobody lead
the likes of us till I arise and come
from the holy city of Delirium.

Nobody knows the trouble that came on.
It wasn't long before I rose and went
and left behind the scent of all that pain
and sped to find that cubby in a tent
of hedgerows leaning green and difficult
beside a yard where other children sat
by toys their stranger mothers found no fault
to let them play with, and I looked at that
thin strip of grass between the dirt and walk.
There came some footsteps falling and I saw
a lady wearing lady-clothes. Her talk
was plain: Boy, she said, if you do not know
the one thing that I told you, listen again:
Learn to disdain the things that want disdain.

I got up toward the breaking of the day
to take my bearings from that broken dream,
but all the streetlamp gave me was a room
much like the one I slept in as a boy,
except the busses didn't run all night
and there weren't any ships braying upriver.
Out where the planets were was dark as ever
for all my lack of motive to look out
and wonder anymore. Whatever they said
was there I took for granted, what was not
was not, and what a man could do I did
about the things I had some say about.
Anything much else was in the mind of God,
even the daybreak, what there was of it.

LITANY AGAINST THE BELLYACHE, UPON ST. BRIGID'S DAY

Then it was the fierce place in my middle
where the crazed flatus was
& with it a prayer to holy Mother Brigid
that she might heal me from her nunnery in the sky
because I suffered nightsweats & burnings at stool
because it was the tea-colored diarrhea
because I was in pain
because there was neither joy in my supper nor bliss in my bedding
because it was Venice all night in my mind
because we two sat watching the vaporetti
because she had hastened to join me after my drunken entreaties
because the vaporetti came back & forth
because none of this was true
because there had been neither entreaty nor hastening
I was too much alone
I was in pain because of my flatus
I was lying awake in the midnight over too much flatus
I spent my last prayer like a hasty letter home
I brought her down to me in a glint of ice-light
where the dour crows perched in the branches
where their broken cries came raggedly down from above
where the Saint looked over the windowsills of joy
where she had come to me anyway true or untrue
where I had told her over again the same brave lunacies
where the blight in my belly sang "Stranger in Paradise"
instead of *Benedictus*
instead of any Sunday by the Grand Canal
nor any vaporetti
but the Rue Saint André-des-Arts in Montparnasse
or the alleys of Iraklion black with crones
or the gray isles west of Inishmore
where never womenfolk ever were nor any thought of them

23

ST. ANTHONY BRINGS ST. PAUL THE HERMIT
A CLOAK IN WHICH TO BURY HIM

—after Sassetta

Nobody ever visits. The cave gets blacker
the longer I try to brighten and warm it
with kindling from the forest over yonder.
Try burning the last cedar bough you gnawed on
and you will perceive the meaning of abnegation.

Great Anthony said he was coming, so here he comes.
His satchel means he has good things to read,
and how many items to do with otherwise?
At least he has journeyed through villages
where sundown brightens the shoulders of young girls.

If I could wrap myself in that cloak of his
just once, and dream all the way to the end
of the ecstasy I usually am wakened from
by the biting chill, maybe she would come
to warm my slumber before going home.

SLUGS

There is an awful kindness in the way this cat
keeps his own counsel about these terrible slugs
curled in his dinner or draped from his waterbowl
or stalled at the end of a strand of belly-drool.
I wouldn't live that way. They would just make me mad.
My heart's in the wrong place. I am not any good
   at putting up with matters of this kind.

These nightly visitations from the Under-Slime,
the Ur-Spittle of the Creation, I couldn't
deal with them, even in my own way, even from
my end of the Cosmos of Animate Being.
They'd have to leave. I'd make their lives unliveable,
pry them with sticks, shove them in dust, send them packing
   back where they came from I can tell you that.

As for the cat, what goes on in his heart of hearts?
Above him in the clouds most of the moon moves by,
while he steps amiably among these least of all
God's negligible beasts, these bloodless gastropods —
one crestfallen cat with his entourage of slugs,
and nothing for it but to hang around my yard,
   with me and my people fast in our dream.

AT THE TIRE FIRE AT THE LANDFILL

Down below in the place where the doomed went to and fro
I bespoke one who had just come from the light of day
still flailing his arms and trembling in the sudden cold
that seeped under his shroud, and gawking around the place.
It wasn't at all the kind of scene he had in mind.
Plenty of people looked happy to have arrived there.
Some of them stood gazing about with arms at their sides,
noses poking the air, eyes bugged open in wonder.
The thing he asked me when he came over was how come
life seemed to be going on as usual down here
among the shadows as above in the light's kingdom?
And why shouldn't there be so many with familiar
points of view, I said; this isn't so bad, I said: no
better and no worse than life in Akron, Ohio.

THE MISSING LINK

I saw this on All-Star Wrestling
It was a man named The Missing Link
First he kicked some other man in the knee about 12 times
& pulled him by the hair into the ringpost
& butted him in the forehead with his own forehead
& knocked him out of the ring
& then he climbed down
& picked up a folding chair & hit him
straight in the face with it
& bowled him over into a row of other folding chairs
with other people in them
& then he went to work and strangled him
so that his eyes bugged out of his head
& then he grabbed him by the hair again
& dragged him back up into the ring
where he laid him out nice and flat
& then he climbed up onto the turnbuckle
& flung himself down on him
until the referee
had slapped the mat 3 times
He was billed as the Man Who Felt No Pain
presumably neither his own nor anyone else's
When I witness events like this
I envision a mighty mindlessness in the Central States area
Or as Augustine puts it
Whence is this monstrousness
and to what end?
Circumspice
The grotesque is everywhere

THE MANHOOD OF IRELAND

One afternoon at Egan's in Kilkee
I show JJ my map of Shannon Estuary.
Look JJ, I tell him, Look at this map:
Here's the River Fergus like a great vas deferens
Pouring its turgid sperm into the Shannon.
Ah 'tis, he says, Ah yes, a true bloody fact,
And turns to talk about the Charolais and the Whitehead Herefords
With Jerry McDermot up the bar.
No JJ, listen to me, I tell him, Look again, look here:
This is the manhood of Ireland plunging
Into that great slut of an ocean.
'Tis that, he says, Yes indeed, I see it there,
And calls for another pint from Clare Egan for each of us
And helps himself to a Woodbine out of Jerry's pack.
Mary Carey comes over,
Dangling a half-glass between two fingers.
And what was this you were mentioning over here JJ, she says.
Mary Mary, let me explain, I say,
We were discussing the virtue of the Whitehead cattle
As compared to the Charolais . . .
Which are a dead loss, says Jerry McDermot.
Oh I see, she says, Oh yes.
Nothing of the kind, Clare tells her,
The infamous Yank is lying to you, Mary:
He and JJ were examining the River Shannon on this map
And how it pours itself into the ocean
In an act of fornication.
Ah go on, says Mary Carey.
A dead loss, says Jerry McDermot.

THE HOUSE OF GOD

Mick has a good time staying home from Church
with me while Mom goes praying with the others.
He likes the preacher in the glass cathedral,
I don't know why. I put a record on
to bring us music in the place of words.
Dvořák is here, the violin concerto.
Mick listens and, for reasons of his own,
he shuts the preacher off. That steely face
darts like a goldfish into the murky tube,
the Lord's man lying blind in his own bowl.
The violin is soaring. It is Josef Suk,
the Maestro's kinsman, carving out the air.
Hulk Hogan is here too, Mick's little man,
flexing his plastic wings from the piano.
Mick, I remind us, we are with the Blest,
the solid citizens of light and song.
There is a sweetness in us not for sale.
Our souls are rich with this the Lord's own musick.
Why should we spend them on the likes of these
who labor to break our hearts and keep the change?
With this, I'm shut from braver utterance,
for lo, behold, the Hulkster is on the wing
like a great beefy bird from Mick's embrace,
and Mick jumps up to meet him in the air
so both of them can tumble down again
released and rescued under Josef's bow.
We are the dancers that the set gives back.
The one blind eyeball of the church of man
looks in and finds us up to everything.

BLACKBIRDS

Coming in from watering the pepper plants,
I watch blackbirds descending from the roof
onto the cat's bowl by the mock orange tree.

They leap and peck at morsels and shake their heads
one at a time like bickering theologians
back in the days of the great heresies
troubling the Empire with anathemas
and disputations over syllables —
homoousion versus *homoiousion* —
that one vowel bringing in the Visigoths,
Alaric and Adolphus and the rest,
delivering Rome itself to frightful plunder.
Honorius, the sitting emperor,
survived a dozen years to sport the purple
while the Empire's fabric "yielded," in Gibbon's words,
"to the pressure of its own weight," weakened within
by murmuring monks and blear-eyed visionaries.

Mommsen would say it was slaves raiding granaries
provoked by water in the Spanish mines
or madmen belching fire and oracles,
which is your basic socioeconomic
formula we hear more of latterly,
and altogether feasible, if we acknowledge
not only what we know about the Romans
but what we see each day in the South Bronx.

At this point, seasonably, I give it up
and head on in to catch the Nightly News
for a homeopathic dose of *mal du siècle*,

but on the way I look up at the blackbirds
back on the roof. They have these looks that say:
We know exactly what is happening —
we know exactly who the fuck we are.
I hope the cat's revenge is merciless.
I think I could turn and live with vegetables,
they are so savory and unperplexed.

THE SUN COMES OUT IN SOUTH HAVEN

As far as I understand him, Bonaventure
believes the human soul is a looking glass,
and when we look at it from the right angle
in the right light, namely the light of Grace,
it shows us the face of God which is a fire
and this fire becomes a fire inside the mind
which thus concludes its journey into God,
forever burning and forever changed
into the image that it caught to start with
from the soul's mirror. The object is to look
inside our souls as deeply as we can
so that we become the light and burn and shine.
Now that the sun is out in South Haven
the beach is crowded with enlightened souls.
If I give the impression of someone
reading Saint Bonaventure at the beach,
that's more or less exactly what I'm doing,
though truthfully the book is in the car
and I'm remembering what I read last night.
I drive here with my wife and kids to seek
delivery from life in nearby Kalamazoo
with its eighty thousand tarnished looking glasses.
I come to South Haven to shine and burn
and contemplate salvation. When the sun
was hidden by the haze, we felt remote
from any godly principle, but now
with the light shining over us again
all of us here are clearly come to light
in new skins to be found by the new eyes
of others looking at them as themselves
resplendent and transformed, as from a fire

involving everyone body and soul.
I ought to have an understanding heart,
but being skeptical and mostly blind
as Bonaventure says I mustn't be,
I have a hard time seeing my own face
plainly, let alone God's, on a good day,
from any angle and in the best light.
If finding God is finally done with mirrors,
then when we move aside God moves aside
so nothing's there but the blank looking glass.

THE JOURNEY TO BRINDISI

hic ego mendacem stultissimus usque puellam
ad mediam noctem exspecto

— *Horace*, Sat. *I.v.*

In the middle of the night I am wide awake
riding through eastern France in an ancient Deux Chevaux
after we have stopped for wine and bread
in a town with rain-black streets and glistening shopfronts
and women in lavender raincoats hurrying to market.

I am in the backseat gnawing the bread
and prying the plastic cork from the bottle
the one time too many
and trying to cheer up everyone with a song
I make up as we go. One of my friends up front

is peering angrily through the wipers' swaths
and struggling to carry us over the Jura
to the Alps and Italy and the ship at Brindisi
while the other stares into the book she has been reading
all the way from Paris. Often it dawns on me

they are having a desperate affair
but nights like this I am perfectly confident
it is plain disdain between them
and palpable lust on my part from the backseat
though I become remarkably drunk

by the time we cross the border at Pontarlier
and must immediately empty myself behind the customs stop
down an embankment over a steep ravine
where invisible cascades go roaring through the night
into the blacker darkness where the mountains are.

LACRIMAE RERUM

et mentem mortalia tangunt
— Aen. *1:462*

It was the slow movement of Beethoven's Violin Concerto
That set me weeping under headphones over Montana once
At 32,000 feet, heading for Portland to meet my love
With more than one martini and a load of grief inside me.

Up there it was me and Heifetz and his honey-sweet Guarnerius,
All of us drawn into such an unhappiness that I was the one
Left weeping so inconsolably I called the flight attendant
To ask if these were the friendly skies I'd heard so much about.

Since that moment I have never again been deeply utterly sad,
Even though, many times, I have dandled misery on my knees,
And certain of my dearest have gone off over into death
And others have been in pain who were precious to me —

But never have I wept such perfect nearly interminable tears
Nor have I ever known the mourning in the midst of things
With such an unspeakable knowledge of how things happen to be
Either above or upon the lost planet we call home.

This wasn't art or gin or maniacal love that drove me down to this.
Neither Beethoven nor Heifetz nor Signor Guarneri & Sons
Nor Hiram Walker nor United Airlines nor the dear lady in question
With her honey lips and thighs and breasts and slippery skin

Had anything to do with the condition I was in. It was The Tears
Of Things — and this is the truth of it: it was The Way Things Are
That I was wakened to for that one moment and never ever again,
Please God, for my own good and for my children's after me.

AMID A PLACE OF STONE

Be secretive, Tom Fool —
Get where the weeds grow
Thin to the hawk's call
Near where the seawinds blow,
And warm what you have kept
Of what you call your soul,
The part that was not trapped
By all their rigmarole
Who would hold your life in check.
Don't let them get your name
Or comprehend that look
You give them when they come,
As endlessly they will,
To find out what you are
And how you keep so full
Of silence and desire.

LIBERTY

— to Patrick Kavanagh

Looking for liberty in common things,
stones by the roadway, white goats on the hills,
and then pronouncing them in syllables
feisty and sad the way a bad man sings
on his way to the noose: *I'm no man's brother
no father's son,* while all about him lean
countrymen clean as whistles, countrymen
clean as countrymen, clean as one another:
Kavanagh, you got even, didn't you.
Once you could sing of nothing to sing of,
out came the song of everybody's love
of nothing but the daybreak in the window
with the black roadway by the gate above
bending on down to the townland below.

HALFWAY IN THE JOURNEY

It was the tall Chinese who gave the dream
its central order, which was oddly absent
till halfway along when all of us recent
arrivals wandered into that glass room.
Eyes looked in from three sides but from the fourth
a row of nervous carbines opened fire
and out came finches drifting in thin air.
The tall Chinese, in accents of the North
understood only by a chosen few,
gave out that we must line up by the wall
to have our eyeballs checked for cholera.
Then we two ended up in a yellow car
careening above the cliffs of Donegal
on our way to a requiem for Tommy Power.

FISHING COW CREEK
DURING THE GRENADA INVASION

Whiskey light is flickering opposite
the sun. Our spinners whistle in the stream
like schoolgirls on streetcorners. It is late
enough to be drunk like this. This daydream
says we have been here in another life.
Over the low-water bridge an open jeep
pokes among shadows glinting from the bluff
like dancing dragonflies. If ever we sleep
and dream of a place like this, it is that other
life we are dreaming from. Across on that side
the top floor of a shop has fallen over
in somebody else's war. The neighborhood
deadbolts its doors against the glint of gun
or handgrenade flickering in the sun.

THE DANCING GROUND

My friend sends me a book inscribed with lines
that set me wondering what else he knows
about the way we choose our chosen ones
and how we draw them into magic bows
each in a separate color of desire,
a different prism for the countless ways
all of them came to be the ones they are.
I see the two of us and our ladies
hand in hand on a dancing ground somewhere
in open country, and our children rise
among us in a clarity of air
to fill the clearing with their dancing cries,
as we go shedding loosely from our bones
the lights we carried in our several skins.

THE DREAM OF '43

I lived in a baronial old house.
It was the spring of 1943.
Something had happened in the family.
Uncle said we have lost the best of us —
may God indeed give them eternal rest.
Which always had to be the final word.
That morning I walked out from Oughterard
to look up Michael Furey's lonely ghost,
I thought there might be more than rhetoric
in Joyce's paragraph about the snow.
I thought of Uncle's line about the light
and how it falls on each of us alike —
how often things we never knew we'd know
come on us in the middle of the night.

THE FUNERAL

Right away I noticed our priest was gone.
I had to go looking for a substitute
in that godforsaken corner of Michigan.
By the lakeshore was a makeshift rectory
whose only resident, a free-lance Jesuit,
said I'd be happy to, let me get my vestments.
We were burying my father for the last time.
Fr. Sylvester Ahearn, S.J., presently emerged
in the alb his mother made him in 1941.
Back at the bier where the coffin used to be
was an empty Jameson case with my father in it
like a blown-up rubber toy deflated and folded,
his flat smile beaming and his left hand,
gloved like a clown's, stuck by the thumb
to his right nostril, fanning the air goodbye.
Beyond him the lake was festoons of lilypads.
Low-lying islands bristled with jackpines.
I thought of Lago Trasimeno near Perugia
where Hannibal destroyed the Roman legions
and Francis wrapped himself in sacred fire
while Jesus flickered in a glint of light
at the forest's edge, beckoning, beckoning.

BABIES, BABIES

The mailman trudges upstreet with his bag of dead cowskin.
Muffled voices of lovers are calling one to one
corner by corner from the neighborhood under his elbow

where numberless dreamers have a dream like this:
We are searching for the lost poet of the Class of 1960,
an angular white-haired professorial angel. He is out

eating scampi with Gloria Cahill. She kicks off one shoe
and shoves her bare foot up the back of his knee.
He contemplates the companion he left elsewhere in a dither.

Outside, the gradual jollity of springtime edges amongst us
in the recondite lunar cosmology intrinsic to the tradition
by which we situate the Resurrection in our calendar.

And the babies, babies, the reeking babies in the back room
speak riddles that form in bubbles with little windowpanes
and sills beginning to cool from the vanished breasts of maidens.

A BOYHOOD AMONG THE CANNIBALS

We had three mean Armenians across the alley.
The eldest had a moustache at eleven.
People said they ate dogs. Some of our dogs
would disappear, and it was the Armenians that ate them,

we knew that. I was positive they ate mine.
Armenia was a place of black defiles and flashing knives.
Catmeat rather than dogmeat was tabu,
dogmeat being the avatar of the god of the Armenians.

Nevertheless we had cats disappear on us as well.
My sister Mary Ann brought home the backbone of a cat
with a bit of tabby fur in a puffball at one end
and barbecue sauce on the other. Pakko, the eldest,

was better behaved than his brothers. He would tip his hat
to my mother as we came up the street
and grin down at me from around his toothpick.
No doubt he had graduated past cats I thought.

THE POSTCARD

Somewhere inside him is a backyard picnic
with uncles in suspenders finding nickels in his ears.
Naturally it is summer. The War is over.
The aunts are happy to have the uncles home.

In the postcard on the nightstand it is 30 years later.
The sky is rumpled linen over the Dunes Hotel.
By brassy light he turns his thumb inside her
like a safecracker working the tumblers.

THE AD HOC COMMITTEE

I was live-in lackey for the General and his nameless companion
at their rambling swampside house,
which was once the Egyptological pavilion
of the World's Fair in Tegucigalpa, Honduras.

This particular afternoon the General
had eased himself into a watery décor of leafage and petal.
Beside him swam a lachrymose yet likable crocodile.
They traded anecdotes in matters military, gustatory, and financial.

Come to find out, they were the ad hoc committee
investigating allegations against the other two of us.
Over and over we protested our liberty
to do whatever we liked in our own house,

not to mention our own backswamp. Which didn't sit well.
They set out to get us in the American Legion Hall,
where we had holed up to drink beer and play pool
and show them what rebels we were, wholly ungovernable.

IN THE FORUM AT LUGDUNUM

I stepped off the bus near a monumental square in the north sector
where there were embassies, banks, archiepiscopal residences,
each giving onto its own garden or vestpocket courtyard

into one of which I disappeared
to find myself on a cinderpath lined with blackened emperors
whose brazen deeds exulted from their pedestals —

the afternoon suffused with rank autumnal light
as of mists and smudgepots someplace in the 7th Century,
its Imperial district an oddity, a weed-grown tourist trap.

I had come to buy a locket to carry your picture in,
and here I was among the oracles of official brigandage.
Not one of them spoke the name I called you by.

IN PROSPECT OF EDEN

Here in the tropics they feed you a kind of pâté
made from the ground flesh of rare white lizards
which can only be hunted at night in the rainforest.
This they serve in little lacquered bowls
along with dishes of spiced oil for flavor
since, no matter how many hours they boil it,
the meat retains a foul aftertaste not unlike
the reek of linen from malarial deathbeds.

I generally dine alone toward late afternoon
on the east side of the verandah facing the orchid garden
and beyond it the first deep foliage of that otherworld
which passes for our image of temporal paradise
or earth's own hell, I can't be certain which.
Some afternoons I am true to what I was told
and can literally see in it both Chaos and old Night,
but there is that in me which views it otherwise.

Lately I have a revery of the Fens — the way they look
on the way in to Cambridge from Nottingham, as the train
rushes among swirling grass — the phlegmatic faces
of water-buffalo peering out, an occasional flicker
from the sleek backs of wildebeest fleeing
and in the next clearing the lioness skulking about
belly to the ground, not five miles from Ely Cathedral,
an hour's prowl from the penetralia of civilization.

Once I found myself in the little church of St. Botolph's
wondering over the tomb of a man and wife from Milton's day:
and what shall we do with the body of this grief, I thought,
and where do we look for mercy afterward?

Later that morning I sat by the Cam and watched two children,
a girl and boy, tossing stones in the dappled shadows.
I knew then I was already profoundly tired of time
and of the strenuous perplexities one can ponder in its name.

And then I saw the darksome Mind in the void
erupt from emptiness like a lava-burst spewn forth
though there was no place out of which it spumed
and nothing under it to settle round.
Here was the place I sat in, and the light was cool.
Beyond an archway, up a sunlit colonnade, music was breaking
like wavelets turning backward over shingles
and next there was that silence before new music.

And I saw the great beast's sunward eye, gathering the light,
becoming an eye filled with so much light of its own
it was all the light there was in that place,
and this light was full of rage — it was a fire
consuming the whole of the world in its terrible hunger,
and I was one of the least things it ravened on,
sweeping me into its slathering maw, till I shook myself loose
and regained the morning and the riverbank and the music.

By then I heard her calling me from the bridge.
The sound of my name came shimmering over the river
like the reflection of her call. I went where she was going
for a long while afterward. On certain evenings
after a rain, I watch the hunters ambling down the road
and I hear her calling me among the parrots' voices
from the low bridge over the marsh on the way in
where the lizards come down to feed and hatch their young.

HERE LIES THE HEART

Place would have had to have been more or less important
or else there would have been no boulevardiers,
no bulbous passersby in wineglasses beside blue ashtrays
redolent with Gauloises, no late afternoons at Les Halles
hunting bifteck for the hotplate back at the room
or nights prowling among *les durs* up and down Pigalle
or mornings waking to shouts and traffic
in the Rue Gît-le-Coeur, with its roofscape of chimneys,
geraniums, cats stepping along gutters six stories up

above alleys and dooryards, domain of the sly concierge,
Monsieur the Innkeeper lighting his briar in the vestibule,
the heady swell of that first step out to the sidewalk
into the raving day. Or so it would seem
in memory's curvature, beyond banality, the mind itself
a fabulous geographer. I have looked out this window,
over here, any number of times, and have seen
the crossroads at Mirtiés on the island of Kálymnos
where the café has a doorway with no door in it

but strings of multicolored beads chittering like crickets.
Behind them a solitary wooden table back in the shadows,
voices in there, high-pitched women's voices yelling out,
while one old man by the front wall out in the sun
at another square wooden table stirs his café turc
with a dull steel spoon. On the windowsill above him
one dusty geranium. Bone-white noontime all around,
and up the mountain of Agios Prophitis Elias, a dry wind
in the cave-mouth where the Saint would climb to pray

midway through life's toil, having given up that need
to find one place toward which the soul keeps tending
by sheer invention, beginning with the idea of place itself,
and thereby finding it, of necessity, and naming it,
in after time, by the name his brethren gave him.
I have no proof that any such saint ever dwelt in that place,
nor any evidence, from this remove, that such a place exists
except by thinking of it now, and in these words. Instead,
I remember another old man at a table, a haggard old fisherman

at the café down by the harbor, where the sponge-boats
rocked at anchor. He had gone off once in his youth
diving hear Africa. Months later when he came home
he was greeted with news of the fire that burned his house
and killed his wife and seven children. From then on
he spent every day in that chair at that café
weeping over a Bible open always to the story of Jonah,
speaking to no one except to tell only the one tale
of how he came home years ago to weep and keep on weeping.

WILLOW

A day like this I feel like telling my neighbor
how supercelestial the look of his willow is

as seen through my front-room window. It's partly
his willow, partly my window, which has curved panes

so there's a goldfish-bowl effect, & also
the splattering of new-green grass, which is

golden of course, this being early Spring
the year of Bach's 300th birthday. I am

listening instead to Mozart's "Paris" Symphony,
K. 297, the one he wrote while Mother was dying,

none of which seems even vaguely important. I live
a completely ramshackle life in the vegetable

midland. Children beleaguer us. Babies awaken us.
Mother & I go to bed around 3 in the afternoon

to partake of some hasty carnal refreshment
while one of the boys is over at the Park fishing

& his brothers lie abed amid stench & toys.
Later I put on the seraphic C-Minor Symphony

for Organ & Orchestra by Saint-Saëns, which the jacket says
is the most glorious evocation of the gusto of God

anywhere this side of Bach, maybe bigger than Bach
whose organ Saint-Saëns' recalls. Later still I have plans

to begin composing my memoir about my Cambridge days
then treat myself to ice cream the way Mozart did

at the Palais Royale the night he gave them
that last allegro, marking his ascent into manhood.

The reason I call this poem "Willow"
has to do with my neighbor's tree in his frontyard

though not entirely. This man is one
who brought only daughters into the world.

When he walks up the street, as infrequently he does,
I note that listing walk of his and consider

how he has walked that way all of his life
& bequeathed his walk to his daughters, charming

ungainly girls who will both of them one day & possibly
for numberless days in a row & as many afternoons

send their husbands into musical hallucinations
the way that willow does, the way the memory

of rose light fluttering above billows of Bach
in King's College Chapel has power to do —

the way her skin invariably will
when I have placed my face above her Islands of Langerhans

& her belly is covered with sweat like a melon
fresh from the fruit-drawer and the company of endive.

THE MORNING MAIL

I gave myself the liberty to stay home
one Monday when I should have gotten dressed
and gone and pulled my end up like a man.
The house got empty after breakfast, which
was normal, though the house stayed empty weekdays,
excepting this one, where there was myself,
almost fanatical about the weather,
halfway determined to be under it,
listening for order in this nasty place
or words for persons not at this address.
After the mailman came and went, it was
the letter from a friend in Massachusetts —
pleading his right to special courtesy
from those among his fellow countrymen
who took the time to soothe him where it hurt
in the worn-out musculature of the soul —
making me lie back down in my bathrobe
to read for evidence of the common life
between us, with our other parts at large.

Outside was twenty years of waking dreams,
as of one rainy Monday in Joigny
at the Café République on the main square
where she kept stirring her café-au-lait
and glancing aimlessly over her shoulder,
wondering why we did this, but why we did
she wasn't to realize till we had crossed
the Alps to Domodossola and the Lakes,
and there, in rain again at Sirmione,
she thought of how it was at home in Hartford
and why she had to go there one day soon.

Later that season, it was rain again
in Athens. Two old men in iron chairs
were leaning head to head above their beads
dangling between them, waiting for the train.
The sun came out in Yugoslavia —
men's voices calling in the stationyard
after a rocking stop at Leskovac —
voices of crickets teeming in the corn.
I kept remembering that murky sunup
on the beach at Kalamaki near Piraeus
after a wakeful night. Down came two women
leading a blind old woman to the water,
and then the three of them, their dresses rolled,
stepped in the water while the old one cried.
Those are her daughters and they're bathing her
was the one thought that horrified us both,
to think of the Aegean as a bath of death,
these godly waters we took refuge by
in one another's arms, I said out loud,
already hearing voices in the room.

The letter dropped behind the davenport
laden with pain beyond my reach. I said:
It's time to rise up and behold the day,
to stand beside the window and behold.
The usual blackbirds on my neighbor's roof
had come to shiver as the rites require.
They were three women, one of them a crone,
leaning together, elbow to elbow,
and one complaining *Sister, she is old —*
we need to take her up and make her fly,
and if she doesn't, maybe she should fall.

And what if they should tumble after her,
leaving their cries to falter in the quiet,
what would they be but black birds tumbling down
to drift above a neighbor's roof again? —
black angels veering in the atmosphere
to look us in our faces where we stand
like empty-handed lovers facing the sea,
wondering why we do this, and how those birds
could fall and keep aloft in the one air.

SATURDAY

The thing I did that morning was I got
Up out of a sound sleep, typically
Rested and overjoyed to be awake
Again — after a dream, this time, of ships
Plying the estuary of the Plate
Laden with weightless ore bound for Toledo,
City of churning skies and striving spires
And saintly rhapsodists in fiery raiment.
The last time I had come this way, in fact,
It was a jumbo-jet bound for St. Louis,
City of Bobby's Creole Restaurant,
Stan Musial and Howard Nemerov —
Three of the monuments of the Modern Age —
And tilting over western Illinois
I thought, How ravenous these vasty plains,
How frail these peopled places in the midst.
Et praesens nullum habet spatium —
Augustine in the deeps of his Confessions
Trying to find the time within the mind's
Own midmost moment in the firmament,
As on a river coiling by nightbound lights,
And telling his soul, My soul, don't make a noise,
Don't move — steady she goes: I'm measuring
The Silence now — the Big One — that which Is,
And you, my soul, are all I get to measure,
But here you are reeling around inside me
In an upheaval of bizarre affections.

Downstairs was Julio Iglesias
Exalting the walls with Time and Time's passing —
Où sont passés mes beaux jours? — hoo hoo — then:
Tiempo, Tiempo, ho ho, hoo hoo —

And there I was, exalted by the moment,
But lately awake, but lately out of bed.
Diurnia, goddess of everyday,
Pulled back the veil that hides her in her slumber
To show me the known world of streets and porches,
And here I was, back in the thick of it,
The omnifarious interior,
An August Saturday in a given year
Of human beings being human beings,
Attending to their daily businesses.
Silentium — we're measuring the silence,
They told me, And we find it long and tall.
Ho ho, hoo hoo. I'm coming down, I said,
I'm coming right on down to see what's up.
There were the blameless babies at their bowls,
There was the mamma in her scant apparel,
Her loose pajama-top of bird's-egg blue.
Bountiful Julio had turned the living room
Into a river full of music, and
Upon that music ships were lilting seaward
Fiery with lovers full of *Gaudium!*,
Hilaritas! — the goodly merriment
That dwells in light, deep in the Omnium,
Companionable light, the light's compadre,
The laughter glinting from the light's own eye —
These lovers catching one another's looks
In light array. *Et age, Domine,*
They sang: *Amemus, dulce fragrantes* —
Julio chanting in silentium:
Remember all the hoppiness we've known —
Amemus et curramus — let us run,
Go out, go on — all of us chanting now,

Some of us dancing, hoppy as we could be,
Reeling about the decks from rail to rail
And going forth over the ocean sea,
Mariners all of us, and admirals
Peering for portals full of pelicans
By rivers emptying their reeky beds
And continents aloose with animals.